ABOUT THE AUTHOR

Jessica Bell is an award-winning author/poet, writing/ publishing coach, graphic designer, and singer-songwriter who was born in Melbourne, Australia. She currently resides in Athens, Greece.

In addition to having published a memoir, four novels, three poetry collections, and her bestselling Writing in a Nutshell series, she has been featured in a variety of publications and ABC Radio National shows such as *Writer's Digest*, *Publisher's Weekly*, *The Guardian*, *Life Matters*, and *Poetica*.

She is also the Publisher of Vine Leaves Press, CEO of Independent Publishing Assistance, a voice-over actor, and the coordinator of the Writing Day Workshops.

In October 2016, she became the new lead singer of the well-known dream-pop group, Keep Shelly In Athens, and records and performs as a solo artist under the name BRUNO.

Visit: *iamjessicabell.com*

polish YOUR FICTION

A QUICK & EASY SELF-EDITING GUIDE

Jessica Bell

Vine Leaves Press
Melbourne, Vic, Australia

POLISH YOUR FICTION
A Quick & Easy Self-Editing Guide

First published 2014 Jessica Bell

Published by Vine Leaves Press, 2019
Melbourne, Vic, Australia

Cover and interior design by Jessica Bell

A catalogue record for this book is available from the National Library of Australia

This book is dedicated to a fabulous man named Blair Hollingsworth, who commented on a Facebook status of mine announcing the title of this book.

He said:
How to Polish Your Fiction
1. Write in Polish
2. Have characters eat pierogies and other Polish foods ...

It made me laugh.
And this dedication was born.

CONTENTS

INTRODUCTION

ABOUT THIS BOOK

First of all, let's not beat around the bush. I must start by saying that this book is designed to help you *polish* your manuscript, not build your story. It can be used as a detailed checklist, so to speak, during your last, or even second-last, editing pass. So if you are reading this book, I am assuming you have reached the last stages of developmental revision, and want to prepare your manuscript for publication (or even submission to a literary agent, if that's the route you intend to take).

In this book, I'm going to show you, step by step, how to polish your manuscript to the best of your ability, on your own, so that when you decide to send it to a professional editor (I always recommend this; a second pair of eyes is gold.) they will have less to edit, and you won't break the bank if they charge by the hour!

So what steps do you need to take to polish your manuscript?

I'm going to make it very easy for you. Below is a list of the points I expand on in this book. I have listed them in the order *I* feel comfortable doing them. You may want to do them in a different order, and that's okay. But I definitely do not suggest you polish style before you are satisfied with your content, because you never know how much text you are going to change. You might well end up changing so much content that you have to double-check you haven't messed up any of your style corrections. It would just be a waste of time.

So without ado, these are the things I'm going to help you polish:

POLISHING CONTENT

- First Line Hook
- Character Consistency & Point of View (POV) Switches
- Dialogue Tags
- Tightening Descriptions
- Chapter Endings
- Removing Superfluous Words
- Identifying & Replacing Tics (Overused Words)
- First Person & Third Person Pronouns
- Tense Consistency
- Line Edits

POLISHING STYLE

- Spelling & Punctuation Consistency (AmE or BrE?)
- Typographical Considerations (Numbers, Time, Quotes & Apostrophes, Dashes, Italics, Paragraph Indents, Spaces)
- Titles & Chapter Headings
- Front Matter, End Matter, Acknowledgements, Back Cover Blurb

You might think there are a few things missing. That's because these are things you should have already mastered by the time you pick up this book. I must stress again, that this book is not going to help you *build* your story. It's all about preparing a polished manuscript.

ARE YOU READY FOR THIS BOOK?

Things you should have already mastered are:
- Plot & Pacing
- Show, Don't Tell
- Incorporating the Senses
- Balancing Backstory
- Eliminating Clichés

But, because I'm a little paranoid, I'm going to ask you some basic questions to see if you have indeed dealt with the above points. If your answer is the opposite of what is in brackets after each question, then you need to revise your manuscript again before using this book. You also may like to ask your beta reader/critique partner these questions to get a more objective perspective on your progress.

PLOT & PACING

- Does it have a clear beginning, middle, and end? (yes)
- Do your characters evolve throughout the story, i.e. do they change? (yes)

- Do your characters encounter obstacles along the way which prevent them from meeting their goals? (yes)
- Do your characters eventually overcome obstacles? (yes)
- Are there any sections of your book which seem to drag? (no)
- Do you ever want to skip over some scenes to get to "the good parts"? (no)
- Do you feel there are any scenes which end too quickly? (no)
- Is your story driven by an underlying question that readers need to know the answer to? (yes)
- Are there any major facets of your story you could remove without affecting your plot? (no)
- Does the major thread get resolved, or at least come to a realistic conclusion? (yes)
- Does the big reveal come close enough to the end? (yes)

SHOW, DON'T TELL

- Can you visualize what you are reading as though it were happening right in front of you? (yes)
- Can you feel the emotions your characters are feeling? (yes)
- Do your characters seem flat and lifeless? (no)
- Have you made your characters real? That is, would your readers recognize your characters if they met them on the street—without you using a lot of explicit exposition to describe them? (yes)

INCORPORATING SENSES

- Is the imagery vivid? (yes)
- When a character touches something, can you feel it? (yes)
- Can you hear the dialogue (and dialects, if applicable)? (yes)
- Can you hear everything your characters are hearing? (yes)
- Can you taste and smell all references to flavour and scent? (yes)
- Are you constantly using the words *see*, *hear*, *touch*, *smell* and *taste*? (no)

BALANCING BACKSTORY

- Are there any instances where you feel you are being told irrelevant information? (no)
- Are there pages and pages of backstory all clumped together? (no)
- Does your story begin with the backstory of the protagonist? (no) If yes, are you sure it's necessary to your plot? (yes)
- Have you peppered necessary elements of backstory throughout your manuscript in relevant places that move the story forward? (yes)
- Does your backstory offer significant insight into your characters' personalities, and is it important to readers' understanding of the plot? (yes)

ELIMINATING CLICHÉS

- Are the actions of your characters often described using run-of-the-mill phrases? (e.g. She is driving me nuts.) (no)
- Are your characters stereotypes? (e.g. an intellectual that wears glasses, or a blonde big-breasted lifeguard) (no) If yes, are you sure they're vital to your plot? (yes)
- Have you identified a unique slant to your story? (yes)

Did you answer all those questions correctly? Yes? Fabulous. Then you are good to go.

Almost.

ONE LAST THING
BEFORE WE DIG IN

Before we move on, there are a few techie things you need to know. They will not, in any way, affect the usefulness of this book, but they are things I want to get out in the open so as to avoid any minor frustrations along the way.

1. Any tips I offer on *Microsoft Word* methods of use are from the perspective of a PC user.

2. If you are a Mac user, most references I make to the *Ctrl* key on a PC can be replaced with the *Command* key on a Mac. If you are a Mac user and encounter any problems with my instructions, a simple Google search will sort you out. I do not describe anything complicated.

3. If you are a Mac user and you write in *Pages* (or if you write in *Open Office* or *Scrivener*), please export your manuscript to a Word document before implementing any of the changes outlined in this book. The reason for this is, not only do you want to avoid any of your formatting changes being lost in the conversion

(I know it's generally safe, but you honestly never know), but any freelance editor, designer, or literary agent will want your manuscript in Word. You might as well be prepared.

4. If you do not want to export your manuscript into Word before making any edits outlined in this book, that's fine and totally your choice, but ... (insert smiley face and strong Australian accent here) ... don't say I didn't warn ya!

PART ONE

polishing CONTENT

1.1

FIRST LINE HOOK

There's nothing more important than starting your story right. So don't forfeit the chance to make sure the first line of your novel really cries for readers' attention.

There are a few points you might like to consider to make your first line the best it can possibly be:

I believe the ideal first line does the following:

1. Poses a question. By this, I do not mean your first sentence should literally be a question; I mean it should introduce a conflict that has the potential to spark readers' interest.

2. Hints at genre.

3. Is not too long. Punchy works best. Think about those infamous six-word stories: *For sale: baby shoes, never worn.* They embody so much complexity in so few words, don't they? Aim for something similarly concise and complex. Think of your first sentence as a complete slice of life. It should conjure vivid imagery and intrigue.

4. Is noticeably related to the plot of your story. Even if a reader doesn't immediately recognize it as such, the connection will dawn on them further into the book.

Before I give you an example of a good first line, let me show you a weak one:

My name is Janet and I don't want to see my therapist.

Okay, let's break this down.

Does it pose a question? Erm … yes, but not a very intriguing one. Something needs to be added for the reader to really want to know why Janet doesn't want to see her therapist. At the moment, I'm not really interested in *why* because it hasn't introduced any conflict.

Does it hint at genre? Possibly. Sounds like Women's Fiction or Chick Lit to me. But honestly, it could be anything. If the next sentence reveals she's a Cyborg with an identity crisis, then I'd be pretty sure it's Science Fiction. But why should I wait until the second line?

Is it too long? Nope. At least it's got that going for it.

Is it heavily related to the plot? I wouldn't know. All I know is that the narrator's name is Janet and she is complaining. Not a very compelling character trait to start off with, in my opinion.

Now that we've got the weak example out of the way, let's move on to the strong example.

The deathcare therapists say, "Die happy, live happier."

Does this pose a question? Yes! Why do people need "death-care therapy?" It's obviously not about offering support for the terminally ill, because why would it reference the after-life? And it's obviously not something only one therapist said, because it's written in present tense to express a general truth. So it must be some sort of slogan. Perhaps it's something that is preached through the media? Is it spiritual in nature? Or do people really get a second chance at life after they die? So many questions. I'm intrigued!

Does it hint at genre? I'd say so. I get a sense of Specula-tive Fiction or Psychological Thriller. Big change from my previous genre assumption.

Is it too long? No. I think this is a great length. It's punchy, to the point, and full of intrigue.

Is it heavily related to the plot? I'd assume so. Why offer something so rich with implication if it has nothing to do with the story? From this first line, I'm assuming that this story is about life, death, and finding happi-ness. And perhaps within a moderately dystopian world.

Now it's your turn. What's your first line? Can you make it better?

Checklist:
1. Does your first line pose a question?
2. Does it hint at genre?
3. Is it short and punchy?
4. Is it related to the plot of your story?

1.2

CHARACTER CONSISTENCY & POINT OF VIEW (POV) SWITCHES

Character trait consistency is very important. For example, if you have one character who constantly swears, and has a tendency to lose his/her temper at the drop of a hat, you do not want your other characters behaving in the same way. If this happens, your characters will blend together, and your readers will have trouble being able to tell them apart. You don't want your readers having to back track to be sure they have understood who is speaking/narrating. They should just *know*. And readers know by identifying your characters from the way they speak, move, and behave. For example, if you are familiar with *The Lord of the Rings*, you definitely know when Sam's talking, and you never confuse him with Pippin or Merry even though they're all Hobbits.

You might think you have sorted this out during developmental revisions, but it's possible you have missed a few nitpicky things, especially if your book is written from multiple POVs. If you want to master the voices of your different characters, you cannot rely on revising your work from beginning to end (or end to beginning as some do). You need to isolate each POV and work on them separately.

Let me tell you a true story to prove how important this step is even when you think you have your characters down pat. While I was giving my latest multi-POV manuscript a final editing pass, I discovered that each and every one of my characters' answers began with "Um … ." Yikes! Not good. So I chose one character to assign the "Um … " to and deleted it from the rest. How had I not noticed this before? (And, embarrassingly, I wasn't the one who noticed: a beta reader did.) It just goes to show there is always something you miss, which is why I recommend hiring a second pair of eyes after self-editing your work. The last chapter of this book is rampant with proof of why this is so vital.

So, what I suggest you do is print out your manuscript, isolate all the POVs into different piles (make sure your pages are numbered!), and skim through them one at a time. While you are doing this, make a list of their prominent character-defining traits and behaviours, and any phrases they use regularly.

For example, let's say your story is told from the perspective of three different characters: Bob, Jane, and Doug. And after skimming their pages, you are left with the following list (this is very simple and refined for the sake of demonstrating my point):

Bob:
- Uses a lot of slang and doesn't pronounce the *-g* on words that end in *-ing*
- Often says, "Dude!"
- Elbows the person next to him when he thinks he has said something funny

Jane:
- Snorts when she laughs
- Always says "No way!" to express surprise
- Chain smokes

Doug:
- Never smiles
- Speaks articulately and intelligently
- Often bites his nails

Okay. Now that you have your list, thoroughly read through each POV separately, to make sure these character traits are consistent from beginning to end. Similarly, eliminate any behaviours that belong to the other characters. I can't stress how frustrating it is reading a multi-POV manuscript where every single character has the same repetitive traits.

On the other hand, please don't over-do it with the repetitive traits. Just because Doug bites his nails, it doesn't mean he has to bite his nails on every single page. Use your better judgment.

Checklist:
1. Print out your manuscript (with page numbers).
2. Isolate all the different POVs.
3. Skim through them one at a time and make a list of repetitive character-defining traits.
4. Thoroughly read through each POV to check for trait consistency.
5. Eliminate any traits that belong to other characters.
6. Ensure you aren't overusing the traits.

1.3

DIALOGUE TAGS

I bet you're sick of hearing about dialogue tags. But I tell you, it makes such a big difference when they are used in moderation. I honestly wish I was more aware of the significant difference it makes when I published my debut novel. I religiously avoid re-reading my debut novel because there are so many mistakes I made in that book which I now advise others against. But we live and learn, right? I'm currently writing my fifth novel and I am still improving and growing as a writer.

I think writers are like bottles of wine. Our creative juices taste better with age.

Right. Dialogue tags. In a nutshell, you don't need them! And if you do need them, "he/she says/said" will suffice. Even if someone is asking a question. Why? Because the actual dialogue, punctuation, and action, should tell all.

Let me give you an example of a passage rife with dialogue tags, and then I will show you how to improve it. If you are a seasoned writer, I very much doubt you write like this, but it doesn't hurt to scour your manuscript one last time to see if there are any unnecessary dialogue tags. Trust me, they sneak in. *guiltily raises hand*

"I can't do it," Sally whined, puffing as she yanked the weeds from the soil.

"Of course you can," Frank replied. "You just pulled it free."

"But I'm getting tired," Sally complained, rubbing her neck.

Now let's eliminate/tweak the dialogue tags to make this example as tight as possible.

"I can't do it." Sally puffed and yanked the weeds from the soil.

"Of course you can," Frank said. "You just pulled it free."

"But I'm getting tired." Sally rubbed her neck.

Okay, this clearly isn't an excerpt from a Great American Novel, but it demonstrates my point. It's tighter, it's clear who is speaking, and the flow is smoother. In my opinion, the only time you need a dialogue tag is when the identity of the speaker is ambiguous. This is going to happen if there is dialogue without any action following it. Which, let's face it, sometimes has to happen. Our characters can't be moving their bodies after every single utterance. And if there are more than two people speaking to each other, a "he/she said" here and there will help the reader keep track of who is saying what. So bear that in mind when you are editing your work.

A word of caution: Don't just remove all dialogue tags without considering how you need to change the content following it. Similarly, if you want to remove a dialogue tag after an utterance that is not accompanied by any action, you may need to add some action for it to be clear who is speaking.

Side note: Some authors choose not to use speech marks. If you are one of those, then more tags might be necessary to distinguish between dialogue and narrative. Regardless, you can still avoid descriptive dialogue tags such as *groaned*, *cried*, *replied*, *asked*, etc. Keep it simple and use *said*. (The lovely Jane Davis has said, however, "This [not using speech marks] really isn't recommended. In a study it has just been cited as one of the main reasons readers give up on a book." Something to keep in mind.)

Checklist:
1. Scan your manuscript for dialogue tags and identify the instances you feel need fixing.
2. Replace dialogue tags with action where possible.
3. Replace descriptive dialogue tags with *said* where you believe necessary.
4. Make sure the description in the tag you removed is still evident in the narrative. If not, identify whether it's needed at all and make a decision to either (a) leave it out altogether, or (b) insert some action.

1.4

TIGHTENING DESCRIPTIONS

Too much description and you risk boring your reader. Too little description and your reader has no environment in which to visualize your characters. But it really is a fine line, and depends so much on personal taste.

Being a poet as well as a novelist, I adore description. And I have to admit, I go overboard sometimes. But my "description binges" are always calculated. And more often than not, I cut them down to at least half the original length. There are two ways you can do this. I suggest you implement both for variety of pace.

1. Identify which parts are purely "decorative" and/or have little or no relevance to your plot and evaluate how important they are to you. You don't need to get rid of them all. Just find a balance you're comfortable with. Trust your instincts. And I say don't listen to that "kill your darlings" drivel. If everyone killed all their darlings, they'd have no family left.

2. Extract a big chunk of description and break it down into rational stand-alone segments or sentences. Then incorporate them into some action.

Look at the following example, for instance:

Action:
"I can't believe Selma's gone." John runs his fingertips along the fence before opening the gate.

Isolated segment of description:
Rusty wire fencing borders the abandoned paddock. The gate is squeaky. It always has been. Selma claimed it kept her alert to trespassers and refused to oil the hinges.

Description segment added to action:
"I can't believe she's gone." John runs his fingertips along the rusty wire fencing that borders the abandoned paddock. He opens the gate. It squeaks like it always has. He's reminded of Selma's refusal to oil the hinges. She said it kept her alert to trespassers.

The final example is great because it does several things. There is action. There is backstory and character info on Selma *and* there is description.

In the grand scheme of things—and this applies to everything in this book—the changes you make are *your* choices. So if you want lots of description, and believe it deserves to be there, so be it. But, I urge you, please don't go on and on for pages about the beauty of Mother Nature in spring. Your readers will just stop reading if the action is interrupted for more than a page. Some say that the limit is two paragraphs, but if, like me, you're a literary author, I think you can get away with one page. At the very most.

So, as well as cutting your description to the level you feel comfortable with, and peppering it throughout the action, how else can you go about polishing it? Don't overuse adjectives and use more strong verbs. The key word here is "overuse." I'm not saying never use adjectives. I'm just saying your writing will be stronger with moderate usage.

Weak example:
The darkness of the thick grey low-hanging clouds made the massive decorative rocks in our backyard look like animated gravestone-giants.

Strong example:
The thick clouds hung low and shadowed our backyard. The decorative rocks doubled in size and morphed into gravestone-giants.

Checklist:
1. Ask yourself: Is your description vital to plot? Does it help you understand character? Is it important to understanding setting?
2. Cut redundant description
3. Pepper description throughout action
4. Don't overuse adjectives
5. Use strong verbs

Thesaurus Tip: If you are using a thesaurus to broaden your vocabulary, look up your words of choice in the dictionary. Be sure they mean exactly what you think they mean and that they make sense in your sentence. Nothing screams "Amateur!" more than a sentence in which the author has clearly used the thesaurus with abandon.

Note: Stephen King says, if you need a thesaurus to find it, you are using the wrong word—but I think that depends on what kind of stories you write—complex plots demand simple writing, whereas simpler plots can take more language complexity.

1.5

CHAPTER ENDINGS

A good chapter ending is like having one mouthful of your favourite food left on your plate, but not yet feeling full, so you go for seconds ... and thirds, and fourths, until you're *so* full you have to force yourself to stop.

For me, the key to a great chapter ending is to introduce a new conflict. It doesn't have to be much; a hint of what is to come in the next chapter will suffice. Nor does it have to be anything groundbreaking. It could be as simple as revealing something that changes readers' opinion about a significant character, or reveals a new motive. Or it could be as complex as hinting at the conclusion to the story, but not revealing enough information for the reader to be entirely sure that's the case.

In other words, end with something that poses a new question, or hints at an answer, for the reader.

You may think it's difficult to do this at the end of every chapter. If so, your chapters might be too short. Could you be mistaking the end of a scene for the end of a chapter?

Chapters do not need to end where a scene ends. You can have multiple scenes in a single chapter. Most authors divide their scenes with a line space, or a centered symbol such as three asterisks.

I advise you comb through your manuscript to locate all the turning points in your story and reorganize your chapters so they end where the turning points begin. On some occasions it might simply be a case of rearranging your sentence order to give your chapter endings more punch.

Have a look at the following examples and consider how much more powerful the second version is as a chapter ending.

Weak chapter ending:
I stare at my computer screen, clenching my teeth, flexing my fists under the desk. I click my email closed to reveal a shot of me and Celeste as teenagers in our murky green school uniforms, her feathery blonde hair teased high enough to nest squirrels, my fringe gelled into a wave big enough to surf through. It was three weeks before I decided to skip tryouts for the football team because she told me she was pregnant and wasn't sure if it was mine. She blew cigarette smoke into my mouth, in the hope I might get turned on and forget about it.

Strong chapter ending:
I stare at my computer screen, clenching my teeth, flexing my fists under the desk. I click my email closed to reveal a shot of me and Celeste as teenagers in our murky green school uniforms. She's blowing cigarette smoke into my mouth, her feathery blonde hair teased high enough to nest squirrels, my fringe gelled into a wave

big enough to surf through. It was three weeks before I decided to skip tryouts for the football team.

Because she told me she was pregnant.

And wasn't sure if it was mine.

What does the second example do? It ends on something that is bound to change readers' opinion of Celeste. And not only Celeste. It could also change readers' opinion about the narrator. For example, the reader might have more sympathy for him now and want to read on to see if he receives any concrete evidence regarding his paternal status.

Sure, the first example triggers this reaction too, but it's definitely weaker. Why? Because this new information is hidden between distracting description, and it makes it sound like something the narrator just thought to mention because he was reminded of it. But by isolating those last two sentences in the strong example, not only does this new information have a more powerful impact, but it also shows it has great significance to the plot.

Checklist:
1. Do your chapter endings pose a new question, or hint at an answer to a question related to your plot?
2. If not, locate the turning points in your story and end your chapters there.
3. If necessary, rearrange the sentence order so that the most impactful information is the last thing you read.

1.6

REMOVING SUPERFLUOUS WORDS

See the words in bold in the examples below? You can get rid of them. Get rid of them all. These words are the most common slippery suckers, because, to put it bluntly, they slip into your work uninvited—and they suck.

For the purpose of showing you what to remove, my examples are simple. Again, not Great American Novel material, but hopefully they'll be quick and easy to comprehend. And even if you're an old pro, double checking these things is not a waste of your time. When in the throes of creativity, words that bog down the flow of your text are not obvious, because you are in writing mode, not editing mode. In writing mode, writers tend to focus on general content, not nitpicky stuff like this.

1. He **is/was** stand**ing** by the door. → He stands/stood by the door.

See the "Tense Consistency" chapter for more information on *is, was*, and *-ing*. But on the off chance you are reading the chapters out of chronological order, I will repeat this: avoid using continuous tenses unless absolutely necessary. Considering example one, nothing changes regarding readers' understanding of the action if the verb is written in its simple form. But it will result in tighter and smoother prose, and that is always a plus.

2. She **can/could** hear the dog howl. → *The dog howls/ howled.*

We don't need to know if your character *can* hear the dog howling when the reader *can* hear the dog howling. Because if the narrator is telling the reader that the dog is howling, the character in the vicinity of the howling dog can clearly hear it, too.

3. She **felt** him stroke her cheek. → *He stroked her cheek.*

    He **saw** the birds fly past his door. → *The birds flew past his door.*

    They **heard** the door slam. → *The door slammed.*

    We **smelt** the smell of flowers wafting through the window. → *The aroma of flowers wafted through the window.*

    I **tasted** salt on his lips as they brushed against mine. → *His salty lips brushed against mine.*

Basically, sense verbs are often not needed, as is demonstrated in example two above. You *could* do away with all of them (feel, see, hear, smell, taste). However, it can sometimes be a bit tricky to determine whether you *should* get rid of them or not. For example, you might want to specify that someone in particular could feel/see/hear/taste/smell something, in which case the sense verb might need to stay, so don't go overboard. Such limitations can sometimes result in heightened creativity and your writing is bound to be better for it.

4.   *She grabbed him* **by the** *arm.* → *She grabbed his arm.*

The word *by* can be removed in most cases. But be careful: if it is part of a transitional phrase, for example, the word *by* will be necessary:

By the time he arrived, I had already left the house.

Similarly, if it is a part of a passive clause, in which the "doer of action" is important, *by* will also need to stay:

The letters were mailed by Julie.

Note: Try to limit your use of the passive voice in fiction. The above sentence would be more effective in its active form: *Julie mailed the letters.*

5.   *She didn't* **even** *know how to open it.* → *She didn't know how to open it.*

The word *even* is rarely necessary. It's one of those words that slips in because we use it naturally in everyday speech. But it doesn't serve any significant purpose in narrative. I say get rid of them all. You may think it's necessary, because it slightly changes meaning, but honestly, in many cases it's not.

Let's say that the sentence before the sentence in example five is something along the lines of this: *Julie picked up her jewellery box.* Now read that before the first sentence in example five. Then read it before the second sentence. Has the meaning changed at all? I can't see it. Always evaluate the instances of *even* in context. You'll be surprised how many you won't need.

6. *The doll **that** she thought she had lost sat on the window-sill.* → *The doll she thought she had lost sat on the windowsill.*

This is a defining relative clause in which the relative pronoun (that) is the object of the sentence. When this is the case, we can do away with the relative pronoun. The same goes for defining relative clauses using *which* or *who*:

*We went to the cinema (**which**) Dan recommended.*
*Bob met a lady (**who**) my sister had gone to college with.*
*The town (**which**) she lives in is famous.*
*The man (**who**) my mother married is from France.*

But don't try to remove *that/which/who* from defining relative clauses in which the relative pronoun is the subject:

I need a job that has flexible hours.

See? Doesn't make sense without *that*, does it?

7. *They **finally** arrived.* → *They arrived.*

If you have used your "show, don't tell" skill well, you will not need to tell the reader that anything has *finally* happened. The actions preceding this action should have already illustrated a delay.

8. All he **really** wanted was her love. → *All he wanted was her love.*

Really? Do we really need *really*? I really don't think so. Again, this stems from something we often slip into casual everyday conversation. Don't bog your writing down. It's not necessary, and it can get *really* annoying.

9. *The kid climbed **up** the tree.* → *The kid climbed the tree.*

You don't need the word *up* when the verb alone describes the upward action. *Climb*, alone, means to *go up*. If the kid was climbing down, however, you would need the word *down*. Watch out for verbs which pair well with prepositions. Sometimes the preposition isn't necessary.

10. *Kit walked **in/out through** the blue door.* → *Kit entered via the blue door* or *Kit left/exited via the blue door.*

If Kit is walking in or out through a blue door, she is either entering or exiting via the blue door. Be careful of piling on the prepositions. They can usually be replaced with strong verbs.

11. *Tom dawdled **over** to the couch.* → *Tom dawdled to the couch.*

Again, you don't need the word *over* when the verb alone describes the action.

12. *Gemma played **out** in the garden.→ Gemma played in the garden.*

We know the garden is *out*. We don't need to be told.

13. *She **just** needed him to sit still. → She needed him to sit still.*

Even if the intent of example thirteen was to show it was the only thing she needed him to do, the word *just* still isn't necessary. We would already be in the moment, and you, as the writer, would have already "shown" the situation playing out, and therefore, this fact should already be evident.

14. *Jack was **almost** at the door. → Jack stood inches from the door.*

*Jack **seemed to** be near the door. → Jack stood near the door.*

*Jack was **somewhat** near the door. → Jack stood near the door.*

You don't want things to *almost*, *somewhat*, or *seem to* happen. Be direct. Readers will have more confidence in the narrative. That said, if the narrator is unsure of Jack's whereabouts, *seem* might be necessary. However, there are still other ways you can word this if that's the case. For example: *I assumed Jack stood near the door.*

This comes back to using strong verbs. Strong verbs are a storyteller's saviour.

15. *He was **so very** handsome.* → *He was so handsome* or
    He was very handsome.

Don't overdo the adverbs. I know that eliminating adverbs is becoming quite the writing craft discussion topic due to an abundance of writers crying "adverbs are bad" left, right, and center, and others passionately disagreeing, but using two in a row is definitely unnecessary in fiction. Removing at least one in example fifteen doesn't change the meaning at all. Be conscious of this. Other common adverb combinations which you might like to keep an eye out for are:

*It's **really very** outstanding.*
*There is **so much more** to it than that.*
*It's **really quite** nice.*
*It's **very much** final.*
*There's **even more** than before.*

The easiest way to remove superfluous words is to use the *Find* function in Word and highlight the selections. You are then able to evaluate each instance to determine whether you can eliminate them. Remember, don't go deleting these willy-nilly without considering whether they have a right to be there. That's because sometimes you need them, as stated in examples three and four.

If you don't know how to use the *Find* function in Word and highlight your selections, follow these easy steps:

1. Go to the *Find* function from the *Edit* menu, or simply press *Ctrl+F*. In Word 2007, *Find* is located in the *Editing* group on the *Home* tab.

2. A *Find* box will pop up. Enter the specific word or phrase you want to highlight into the *Find what* bar.

3. Click the *Find in* button below the bar, and select *Main Document*.

4. You will see that all these words have been selected. Be careful not to click inside the document, otherwise these selections will disappear. Go to the *Font* group by either pressing *Ctrl+D*, or by locating the *Font* group in the *Home* tab. Click *Text Highlight Colour* and click on a colour. Now your selected words will be highlighted throughout your manuscript.

5. Once you've edited your selected words, *Select All* (*Ctrl+A*), and click *Text Highlight Colour* under *Font*, and select *No Colour*. This will remove the highlighting from any words you did not change.

Important Note: Do not use the *Reading Highlight* function in the *Find* box. It highlights all the words, but as soon as you edit one thing in your document, all the highlighting disappears.

Find and Highlight Tip: Be sure to include a space before and after the word you are searching for in order to avoid words that contain these letter combinations. For example, *can* would be highlighted in *scanner*.

Checklist:
Check for the following words:
1. almost
2. by
3. can/could
4. even

5. feel/felt
6. finally
7. hear/heard
8. in
9. ing (do not insert a space before this)
10. is/was
11. just
12. out
13. over
14. really
15. see/saw
16. seem
17. smell/smelt (AmE: smelled)
18. so
19. soon
20. that
21. taste/tasted
22. up
23. very
24. which
25. who

1.7

IDENTIFYING & REPLACING TICS (OVERUSED WORDS)

Writers often develop tics, i.e. words we use instinctively. Every writer has them. If you think you don't have any tics, then you've either been aware of them for a long time and consistently work toward eliminating them, or you haven't discovered them yet.

My prominent tics are *just*, *look*, and *scoff*.

The best way to find out what your tics are is to go to *Wordle. net* and paste your manuscript into the box and click *Go*.

Easy.

Wordle.net will create an image that looks something like the image on the opposite page.

nods
put getting stare long
laughs stupid weight nod
feel give need find another fuckin
Yeah arms
heart looks thought
sit fingers fuck laugh
feet Mum something
Oh stop leave
hold anything always throat er help eyes time
next
inside Maybe right Dad tell
deep mouth Sonia door really top
smiles smile bed hard
go face one phone
stand little make come
pull Mick's Ibrahim car bag step back want let
man cheek
front head Mick lip room
take left open enough see Shit
life hand good
mother think Summer
now never
stomach Karter
behind like toward
get just Mia
kitchen even might
bit fucking around going
air close breath Chapter
know trying floor
ask ya Nash got
voice day
makes side look Celeste still try
gonna keep Fuck last thing hear
nose moment school hands maybe
hair without
Just away way mean house
table call
turn sure
two much

It identifies the words that are used the most often, and creates a Word Cloud with them. As you can see, some words are bigger than others. The bigger the word, the more frequently it has been used. There are obviously character names in here, which in most cases won't be easy to eliminate, but it doesn't hurt to double-check all are necessary.

Other evident tics in this manuscript (from most frequent to least frequent) are: *like, just, know, back, don't, think, get, head, eyes, look, want, hand, one, going, something, face, right, even, really, door.* The rest, in my opinion, are not frequent enough to worry about.

Follow the same "find and highlight" procedure as outlined in "Removing Superfluous Words" to deal with your tics. Remember, you don't need to change them all, just balance things out.

Note: *Wordle.net* requires Java to run. Just click "run" to make it work. It's not necessary to download anything. Alternatively, Google "free word cloud creator" to find various other sites if you are worried about clicking on any Java prompts. There are plenty.

Checklist:
1. Upload your manuscript to *Wordle.net.*
2. Save your Word Cloud.
3. Write a list of words you need to reduce the frequency of.
4. Use the "find and highlight" method to flag the words in your manuscript.
5. Evaluate each instance and change them in any way you deem appropriate.

1.8

FIRST PERSON & THIRD PERSON PRONOUNS

Something I see so much—even in my own writing!—is the repeated use of pronouns to begin sentences. Depending on the story, this can result in tedious—and what seems like repetitive—reading, which sounds like this: *So this happened. And then this happened. And she did this, and then he did that.* I'd try to vary sentence structure as much as possible.

When you were a kid, did you ever go to the "milk bar" to buy a bag of "mixed lollies"? I did. Back in the early 1980s. Maybe it was just an Australian thing, so let me explain. How it worked was, they had a buffet of lolllies (candy), and you decided how much you wanted to spend, and the cashier would put in, for example, two of each kind. There were usually about ten different kinds. (My favourites were called *acid drops*.) My point is, think of each scene like a bag of mixed lollies. Vary your sentence structure so that you don't end up with a bag full of fruit gums and no acid drops.

Compare the two versions below. The second version is so much better.

Weak example:
I grab my black tracksuit, the one with the writing on the butt that says Lick Me, *from my dresser drawer. I dress, facing away from the mirror, lower myself to the floor, lie on my stomach, and stare under my bed—the chocolate abyss. I will get sucked in if I'm not careful. And once I'm in, I can't get out until I've eaten everything. I shouldn't even buy chocolate in the first place. But I haven't gotten as far as that yet. Buying it isn't the ultimate problem. Buying it doesn't mean it has to be eaten. I can throw it away any time I like. Honest.*

Strong example:
The most comfortable thing for me to wear right now is my black tracksuit. The one that says Lick Me *on the butt. I put it on, facing away from the mirror, then lower myself to the floor, lie on my stomach, and stare under my bed—the chocolate abyss. If I'm not careful, it will suck me in. And once I'm in, there's no escaping until I've eaten everything. The key is not to buy chocolate in the first place. But I haven't gotten as far as that yet. Buying it isn't the ultimate problem. Buying it doesn't mean it has to be eaten. In fact, any time I like, I can throw it away. Honest.*

The strong example has only one sentence beginning with *I*, compared to the weak example, which contains five. That's a massive improvement.

Again, use the "find and highlight" function in Word to flag *I, He, She, We,* and *They,* and evaluate each instance separately.

Find and Highlight Tip: To avoid highlighting these letters when they appear within other words, such as *there*, you need to include the first capital letter and the space following the word, in the *Find what* bar. Then click the *More* >> button, and select *Match case*.

Checklist:
1. Locate all your first and third person pronouns.
2. If they appear at the beginning of too many sentences in a row, change to your taste.

1.9

TENSE CONSISTENCY

Grammar. Yuck. I know, I know. But getting it right is really important because, if not done properly, it can mess with a reader's comprehension of the text.

For example, I was reading a manuscript recently, where the immediate narrative was written in Past Simple. But there were flashbacks inserted here and there. And the tense didn't change to Past Perfect, as is generally done. I had no idea I was reading a flashback until a person who was dead in the immediate narrative started talking. It jolted me right out of the story because I had to back track and reinterpret what I'd just read.

The lesson? You need to switch tenses if you are going to move backwards and forwards in time. Here are some general rules. I know rules suck. And they are meant to be broken. But let's start with a few so we can talk about breaking them with skill.

1. If you are writing in Present Tense, any references to the past are generally written using Past Simple.

Frank has a red car. (Present Simple)
Frank had a red car. (Past Simple)
Frank drives his red car like a maniac. (Present Simple)
Frank drove his red car like a maniac. (Past Simple)

2. If you are writing in Past Tense, any references to the past before the past in the immediate narrative, are generally written using Past Perfect.

Frank had a red car. (Past Simple)
Frank had had a red car. (Past Perfect)
Frank drove his red car like a maniac. (Past Simple)
Frank had driven his red car like a maniac. (Past Perfect)

This basic rule, however, varies, as there are all sorts of other related tenses you have to consider—Present Perfect, Present Continuous, Present Perfect Continuous, Past Continuous, Past Perfect Continuous, and things like modal verbs such as *would have* and *might have*, and phrases like *used to*. But all this is a bit complex to talk about without giving you a fully-fledged grammar lesson. And, in the context of this book, that would not be "quick" or "easy." Instead, I will give you two excerpts of the same content, each written in a different immediate narrative tense, so that you can see how the tenses change and relate to each other. Most of the time, if your mother tongue is English, the correct grammar will come naturally. But be careful when writing in Present Simple, that you don't refer to the past using the Past Perfect, because it will sound weird.

For example:
Wrong: *Frank has a red car. Last year, he had had a blue one.*
Correct: *Frank has a red car. Last year, he had a blue one.*

Without further ado, read and compare these excerpts. The bold words are your focus.

Present Simple Immediate Narrative:
*The wind **howls** and **rattles** the front door. Rain **pelts** down. Mia and I **look** at the ceiling with our mouths open. But then it **stops**. Typical Melbourne weather.*

*I **hold** a cigarette in the air. A peace offering.*

*Mia **drags** her feet across the carpet. A sound I associate with the Rottweiler we **had** when my ex-wife, Celeste, **was** still around. **Before** she **discovered** she **could have** the life **she'd** always dreamed of if she **hooked** up with that dirtbag plastic surgeon from LA, instead of roughing it out with a high school Phys Ed teacher with a fragile ego—me. I guess what Celeste **failed** to realize **was** it **wasn't** my fragile ego which **messed** us up. We **were doomed** the day Celeste **decided** Ibrahim—my then best mate—**was** going to be our best man.*

*Mia **snatches** the cigarette from my fingers and **sits** next to me. The leather couch **sinks** with a sigh. I **turn** to her, head still hanging, tilted to the side, **preparing** to ask the dreaded question.*

Past Simple Immediate Narrative:
*The wind **howled** and **rattled** the front door. Rain **pelted** down. Mia and I **looked** at the ceiling with our mouths open.*

*But then it **stopped**. Typical Melbourne weather.*

*I **held** a cigarette in the air. A peace offering.*

*Mia **dragged** her feet across the carpet. A sound I **associated** with the Rottweiler we'd **had** when my ex-wife, Celeste, **was** still around. **Before** she'd **discovered** she **could have had** the life **she** always **dreamed** of if she **hooked** up with that dirt bag plastic surgeon from LA, instead of roughing it out with a high school Phys Ed teacher with a fragile ego—me. I guess what Celeste **had failed** to realize **was** it **had not been** my fragile ego which **messed** us up. We **were** doomed the day Celeste **decided** Ibrahim—my then best mate—**was** going to be our best man.*

*Mia **snatched** the cigarette from my fingers and **sat** next to me. The leather couch **sank** with a sigh. I **turned** to her, head still hanging, tilted to the side, **preparing** to ask the dreaded question.*

Notice I have not changed the verb "to be" into Past Perfect. If I did, it would sound too clumsy. For example, *my then best mate—**was** going to be our best man* would become *my then best mate—**had been** going to be our best man.* Yuck, right?

Note: Most sentences only need ONE of the verbs converted to Past Perfect—there are exceptions, but typically that is the norm.

So keep an eye out for this. Make sure any references to the past do not blend in with the immediate narrative, otherwise readers aren't going to know what is *now* and what was *then*.

But don't worry *too* much about this. When you hire that second pair of eyes, he/she is bound to fix any grammar glitches for you. Right now, you need to be concerned with making your editor's job as easy as possible. I will tell you how to go about this in a minute, but you need to know one more thing before I do—about successfully breaking these rules.

Some authors like to use different tenses for different POVs. While I have experimented with using First Person for one POV and Third Person for another in the same manuscript, I have never attempted to alter between narrative tenses. For example, perhaps one POV is telling their story as they remember it in the Past Tense, and another POV is represented in real time in the Present Tense. But they're both still talking about exactly the same time, just from a different perspective. It's a little bit like watching a flashback in a movie—you can see it and experience it as it happens. If done well, it is a great way to add extra dynamic to your story. A recent book I read did this brilliantly. If you'd like to see for yourself, it's called *In the Path of Falling Objects* by Andrew Smith.

But we're not done here yet. I have few less intensive tips:

1. When writing in Present Tense, watch out for the excessive use of *is*, and if you are writing in Past Tense, watch out for excessive use of *was*.

For example, instead of:

*Sheila **is/was** so in love with John she can't/couldn't imagine life without him.*

Change it to:

*Sheila **loves/loved** John so much she can't/couldn't imagine life without him.*

Combing through your manuscript for *is* or *was* might also help you identify actions that are better off being shown rather than told.

For example, instead of:

Sheila is/was very tired.

You could change it to:

Sheila's eyes fluttered as she fought off sleep.

That brings me back to STRONG VERBS. A writer's saviour, see?

2. It would also help to search for instances of *had had*. Too many instances of this and your writing will sound like a tongue twister.

Use the "find and highlight" function in Word to flag *is/was* and *had had*, and evaluate each instance separately.

Find and Highlight Tip: Include spaces before and after each word in the *Find what* bar.

3. As I explained in "Voice Consistency & Point of View Switches," you are going to have to isolate your POVs and make sure you use the same tense throughout each POV. You might wish you had done this at the same time as you were editing voice, but trust me, if you had, you would have had to try focussing on two things at once, which would have resulted in errors. Tried and tested!

Checklist:

1. Can readers make a clear distinction between *now* and *then*?
2. Are there too many instances of *is/was* and *had had*?
3. Are your tense uses consistent within each POV?

1.10

LINE EDITS

This is the last step in polishing your content. Please don't freak out. You don't have to read through your story *again*. Because you can have it read *to* you.

The best way to find out if your sentences flow is to listen to your work being read aloud. If you want to read it to yourself, kudos to you. You will have a much better chance of finding glitches in flow by pretending that you are reading your book in front of an audience. If you stumble over words, you will know exactly what needs fixing. But, you don't have to read it to yourself if you don't want to. There are a few other options.

Option 1:
If you have a Kindle, upload your manuscript and use the text-to-speech function. It might sound a little robotic, but if your story flows well with a monotone voice, it has a lot going for it. To do this, you can either connect your Kindle to your computer via a USB cable, or email it to your free Kindle address.

If you don't know what your free Kindle address is, here's

how you can locate it in your Amazon account.

1. Go to Amazon and click on *Your Account*.

2. Under *Digital Content*, click on *Content and Devices*.

3. In the pane just under the search bar, click on *Preferences*.

4. Scroll down and select *Personal Document Settings*.

5. The first sub-heading you will see is *Send-to-Kindle E-Mail Settings*. Below that it should have your free email address listed. However, be sure to add your personal email address to the *Approved Personal Document E-mail List*, otherwise Amazon will reject the document.

If, for some reason, you don't have a free Kindle address, and you want one, contact Amazon to enquire about it.

Option 2:
Go to *Ivona.com/en/mini-reader/*. This is a free trial of a text-to-speech software. It sounds quite robotic, too, but you'll have the choice of a British or American accent and either male or female voices. It serves its purpose well and is easy to use. Once you've installed the software, an *IVONAReader* tab will appear in Word. All you need to do is open your document, click on the tab, and click *Read*. If you want specific sections read to you, just select that text, and *IVONA* will only read that section. The downside is you have to subscribe to their newsletter to download the free 30-day trial, but that is a small price to pay if you ask me. And if you like it enough

to purchase it, the cheapest option is about $60 USD for one voice. It costs more with each extra voice.

Option 3:
Go to *Naturalreaders.com*. This is a totally free online text-to-speech service. The website is user-friendly. All you have to do is upload your document, choose a voice and reading speed, and hit play. The downside to this version is that it sounds even more robotic than Options 1 and 2. But if you don't mind that, it's a decent solution.

Option 4:
Have a friend read it to you! You can always make it fun. Invite them over for dinner, have a few glasses of wine, offer them a thank you gift. You never know, they might love your book and give you your first five-star review!

If you're not too keen on any of these options (though I really do recommend you try one), you can always do it the old-fashioned way—on paper. If you are going to do this, I suggest you start at the end of your manuscript and work backwards to avoid getting caught up in the narrative and losing focus. The whole point of doing a line edit is to be certain the flow of each sentence is as best it can be. By this stage in the editing process, you do not need to check whether the story makes sense, you need to check the rhythm of your words.

Checklist:
1. Have you listened to your work being read aloud?
2. If not, have you given your manuscript a line edit from end to beginning?

PART TWO

polishing STYLE

2.1

SPELLING & PUNCTUATION CONSISTENCY (AmE OR BrE?)

SPELLING

What is AmE and BrE? They stand for American English and British English, and technically you should use one or the other.

I say "technically" because my own situation is a little odd and I choose to do things a bit differently. I am Australian, which consists of a mix of both AmE and BrE. And because I now live in Greece, and write and edit books for teaching English as a foreign language, and am currently working for a publisher that uses "Global English," my English style is all over the place.

Depending on what, and for whom, I am writing, I might spell things the way the British do (colour), sometimes the way Americans do (color); sometimes I'll use words that only British use (jumper), or words only Americans use (sweater), and when I write with Australian slang (fairdinkum!), some people have no clue what I'm on about. But that's me. And I don't intend to change my style because books say I'm supposed to.

I do, however, follow my own rule: whichever spelling I choose, I make sure I use it the exact same way throughout the manuscript. If you're an expat like me, consistency is key. Write it on your forehead. Remember, also keep consistent within specific styles. For example, don't spell *color* without the *u* and then *favourite* with the *u*.

But enough about being a word rebel and messing with the English language. If you'd prefer to edit by the book, I suggest you invest in a great dictionary and style guide that is written in your English style of choice. This will help you sort out any issues you might have. If you were born and bred in either America or Britain, I doubt you will have any trouble conforming to style, but if you're an expat, it's great to have a reference book handy in case you're unsure about something. If you are Canadian, Australian, or from New Zealand, you can acquire reference books specific to those countries too.

Common differences to watch for between BrE and AmE are:

1. Use of *ou* vs. *o* (e.g. favour/favor, colour/color)

2. Use of *ise* vs. *ize* (e.g. realise/realize, organise/organize)

3. Use of *t* vs. *ed* in past tenses (e.g. learnt/learned, spelt/spelled)

4. Use of *re* vs. *er* (e.g. centre/center, litre/liter)

5. Use of *ogue* vs. *og* (e.g. catalogue/catalog, analogue/
    analog)

6. The dropped *e*, though often interchangeable (e.g.
    likeable/likable, ageing/aging)

7. Double consonants (e.g. travelled/traveled, focussed/
    focused)

8. Unique spellings (e.g. mum/mom, pyjamas/pajamas)

9. Word differences (e.g. jumper/sweater, footpath/side-
    walk)

10. Colloquialisms (e.g. Are you having a laugh?/Are you
    for real?)

For a sufficient free list, you can visit *en.wikipedia.org/wiki/
American_and_British_English_spelling_differences*

PUNCTUATION

You may think it's strange, but punctuation also differs
between styles, so it's good to get a handle on this to maintain
consistent usage throughout your work. Though I generally
use BrE spelling (with a touch of AmE), I really don't like the
BrE use of punctuation, so I stick with the AmE use. Again,
it all comes down to consistency.

Here is the nitty-gritty:

In AmE ...

... "double quotation marks are used"

... "periods, commas, and other punctuation marks, appear inside the quotation marks," they say.
"Are you having a laugh?" the Brits said.
"No."

In BrE ...

... 'single quotation marks are generally used, though double quotation marks are becoming trendy'

... 'full stops, commas, and other punctuation marks, appear inside the quotation marks if the quoted item is a full sentence that ends where the main sentence ends.' But 'most of the time', the punctuation appears outside the 'quotation marks'.

Personally, I don't think that looks very pretty because that means, in 'this sentence', the comma goes outside the quotation marks. The reason I use AmE punctuation in my own books is because I think BrE punctuation looks untidy. But that's totally subjective. If you don't mind the look of it, go for it. Which brings me to using quotes within quotes. According to the styles demonstrated above, in AmE you would use single quotes within double quotes, and in BrE you would use double quotes within single quotes.

And if the quote within a quote falls at the end of a sentence?

Tricky. And it always confuses me. But this is how it should look:

"AmE quote within a quote, at the end of a sentence 'looks like this.'"

'BrE quote within a quote, at the end of a sentence "looks like this".'

'But if the BrE quote within a quote, at the end of a sentence is also a full sentence, it "Looks like this."'

I'll talk more about quotation marks in "Typographical Considerations."

One more thing. Calendar dates are also formatted differently between AmE and BrE:

In BrE, the day comes before the month. The day comes at the beginning, and the year comes at the end. No commas are used except after the day.

Friday, 18 April 2014

In AmE, the month comes before the date. The day at the beginning, and the year at the end. Commas are used after the day and after the date.

Friday, April 18, 2014

There are other variations, such as using a decimal point (.) to divide digits, or an oblique (/). But it would look very odd, in my opinion, to write out dates like this in a fiction manuscript, so I'd just stick to writing it out in full.

Australians, however, don't use dates. We just mark off the days inside the walls of our cave as the sun sets, drink beer, and have boxing matches with kangaroos ...

... just kidding.

Editing Tip: If you are like me, and use a mishmash of English styles, it will save you and your freelance editor a lot of time if you write up a style sheet. That way they have a clear brief to follow. And it will save you a lot of time changing things back if your editor works strictly to AmE or BrE.

That was a hard lesson learned for me when, after receiving a manuscript back from a hired editor, I had to change things like *Mom* back to *Mum*, and reinstate all the phrases specific to Australians because she had changed them to "what is usually said in the States," despite my characters being Australian. Sure, this particular character lived in the States, but just because someone lives in the States, it doesn't mean she should suddenly speak like an American.

Checklist:
1. Choose your spelling and punctuation styles (AmE, BrE, Canadian, Australian, New Zealand, or your own mix of rules).
2. Invest in a good dictionary and style guide written in your chosen English styles.
3. Make style consistent throughout your manuscript.

2.2

TYPOGRAPHICAL CONSIDERATIONS (NUMBERS, TIME, QUOTES & APOSTROPHES, DASHES, ITALICS, PARAGRAPH INDENTS, SPACES)

There are so many of these nitpicky things to consider, so I am just going to focus on the common ones, otherwise I'd end up writing a fully-fledged style manual. To be honest, for fiction, you are not going to have much to think about—it is not a scientific research paper. And as long as you are consistent in the way you choose to style things, you are good to go, in my opinion. I do, however, have a pet peeve with straight quotes, which I will talk about.

NUMBERS

Believe it or not, there are rules for these. In academic texts, the general rule is to spell the numbers out from zero to nine, and to use digits from 10 upwards. The norm in fiction is that one to one hundred appear in the written form and 100+ appear as numerals. Compounds (such as twenty-one) are always hyphenated. Personally, I think it looks odd using digits in fiction, especially if the digit appears at the beginning of a sentence. So in order to simplify things, I'd recommend sticking to words for basic numbers. Unless, of course, you are writing a mathematic equation. Chapter headings and time references are also an exception. For example, I'd prefer, *She is twenty years old*, rather than *She is 20 years old*. But if I needed to have the number 1,235,524, I would definitely not want to spell that out. So just use your common sense.

Even if you adopt a variety of styles, that's okay, but be consistent with your own rules. For example, you might like to use words for numbers that do not exceed two words (e.g. *twenty-two, one hundred*), and digits for numbers that do exceed two words (e.g. *120*).

It's easy to locate and fix any digits that have slipped in if you don't want them there. You don't have to do a "find and highlight" for every single number. Just search for 0 to 9, and then any numbers that consist of two digits or more will eventually be highlighted too. If you want to change words to digits, however, that's a bit more effort. Do you really want to attempt that? I'd say just stick that on your style sheet for your freelance editor to do.

TIME

There are various ways to refer to the time. But it would do you good to choose a style and stick to it.

Various styles include:

Midnight, 12 am, 12am, 12:00 am, 12:00 AM, 12:00 a.m., 12 pm, 12pm, 12.00 pm, 12.00 PM, 12.00 p.m., Noon, Midday, 12 o'clock

Don't forget there is also the 24-hour clock to consider. For example, *1 pm* on the 24 hour clock is *13:00*, in which case the *pm* isn't necessary.

Just remember to make sure you are being consistent. This can get a little complicated if you have a lot of time references in your manuscript, because there isn't anything you can search for which is going to guarantee you catch each and every one. I suggest you choose a style and add it to your style sheet for your editor.

QUOTES & APOSTROPHES

We've reached my pet peeve. Those ugly straight quotes. Yes, there are two types of quotation marks: curly quotes and straight quotes.

Curly quotes look like this:
"Curly quotes are pretty."

The apostrophe looks like this:
It's a pretty curly apostrophe.

Straight quotes look like this:
"Straight quotes are ugly."

The apostrophe looks like this:
It's an ugly straight apostrophe.

If for some reason your Microsoft Word is set to type straight quotes, I advise you change it. Here's how:

Note: The method might vary for different versions of Word, but it's pretty easy to Google instructions. Just search for "how to change straight quotes to curly quotes in Word" and you will find what you're looking for.

1. Click the *Microsoft Office Button* (the button at the top left of your screen which has the red, blue, yellow, and green Microsoft logo on it) and then click *Word Options* (it's the first button at the very bottom of the dialogue box).
2. Click *Proofing*, and then click *AutoCorrect Options*.
3. Click the *AutoFormat As You Type* tab, and under *Replace as you type*, select the *"Straight quotes" with "smart quotes"* box.

If your manuscript is rife with straight quotes and you want to replace them, you can just use the *Find and Replace* function:

1. Make sure you have changed your quote style preferences as I have instructed.
2. Press *Ctrl+H* to open the *Find and Replace* box. Type " in both the *Find what* and *Replace with* bars, and click *Replace All*.
3. Go back to the *Find and Replace* box and type ' in both the *Find what* and *Replace with* bars, and click *Replace All*. This will sort out all your apostrophes.

Important Note: If you are using BrE punctuation, you are going to have a problem replacing all your single opening quotes because then all your apostrophes will reverse. For single opening quotes that do not start on a new line, you need to add a SPACE before the single quotes in both the *Find what* and *Replace with* bars. For single opening quotes that begin on a new line, you need to add a paragraph mark. You can insert this by typing *^p*.

DASHES

Some people use the en dash – with spaces on either side – which in my opinion can make typesetting messy. The reason I think it's messy is because you run the risk of it ending up dangling on the end of the right margin during the designing of the paperback. It can be fixed, but it's a pain in the butt. However, each to their own.

I like to use the em dash—without spaces on either side—I think it looks cleaner. Plus it won't end up dangling on the end of the right margin during typesetting because there are no spaces for it to separate.

Be careful you don't end up using hyphens instead of dashes. Not only is it wrong, but it looks really weird, especially if there are no spaces on either side-like this. Because then you have created a new word: *side-like*.

Can't figure out how to type these? You can select your dash preferences in the same place where you changed you quote preferences. Just select *Hyphens (--) with dash (—)* box. Once this is done, all you have to do is type one hyphen with spaces on either side for Word to automatically change it to an en dash, and two hyphens with no spaces on either side for Word to automatically change it to an em dash.

Tip: If for some reason you want to reverse a single automated change straight afterwards, all you have to do is press *Ctrl+Z* and it will undo.

Please choose a dash style and keep it consistent. I once read a self-published book that had weird hyphen/dash glitches that looked something like this:

Once upon a time —and a great time it was-there was a little girl named Sarah.

Not pretty.

ITALICS

In fiction, italics are generally used for internal dialogue, especially in third person narratives when the internal dialogue is written in first person. In my debut novel, which was written in first person, I used italics for internal dialogue, too. But looking back, I realize I didn't have to because the whole book, bar spoken dialogue, is an internal thought. Honestly, it's up to you. But however you do decide to use italics, like all typographical considerations, make sure you are consistent with it.

Italics are also used if something needs to be *emphasized*, for foreign *lexis*, and for free-standing words such as titles of books, magazines, movies, TV shows, etc. Italics are also used for written texts, such as a letter, as well as text messages on a phone (SMS).

Note: If a word needs to be in italics within a sentence that is already in italics, such as an internal dialogue, then you would change that specific word back to normal.

PARAGRAPH INDENTS

DON'T USE TABS TO INDENT YOUR PARAGRAPHS!

Sorry, for the caps, but I really had to make that clear. If you use tabs to indent your paragraphs, they won't transfer over to any design programs for typesetting a paperback, nor will they convert properly for your eBook.

It's very important that you set up an automatic indent. Here's how in Word (remember if you have another version of Word, it's easy to Google):

1. Open the *Paragraph* dialogue box in the *Home* tab.
2. Under *Indentation*, click on the drop down menu called *Special*, and select *First line*.
3. Next to that, insert *0.2"* in the *By* box, and click *OK*.

Tips:
1. 0.2 inches is an ideal indent size for paperback and eBook.
2. It's customary NOT to indent the first line of a new chapter or section. Paragraphs should only be indented if there is another paragraph preceding it.
3. Please do not use line spaces to separate paragraphs in fiction. It's common for nonfiction, but in fiction it just wastes space. Especially when you have a lot of dialogue together, as each utterance generally starts on a new line.

If you already have a manuscript full of tabs, not to worry, you can fix it pretty easily.

1. Just go to the *Find and Replace* function (*Ctrl+H*) and type in *^t* (that's the symbol for a tab) in the *Find what* box. Leave the *Replace with* box empty and click *Replace all*. Now all your new paragraphs will have moved to the edge of the left margin.

2. Select All (*Ctrl+A*). Follow the procedure on how to set an indent.

3. To remove the indent from the very first line of a new chapter or section, go to the start of each chapter or section, and click the cursor at the beginning of the first paragraph. Follow Steps 1 and 2 in the procedure on how to set an indent, but select *None* instead of *First line*.

SPACES

Gone are the days when we hit the space bar twice after a full stop. It's just not done anymore. But if you do think you have done this, you can easily replace the two spaces with one by using the *Find and Replace* function.

Also, for some reason—and it happens to me too—you end up with an extra useless space at the end of paragraphs. It's a good idea to clean this up before typesetting or formatting for eBook. All you have to do is replace *.[space]^p* with *.^p* and they will disappear.

Note: Do not literally type *[space]*, it means to press the space bar.

Checklist:
1. Have you standardized your use of numbers?
2. Have you standardized your time references?
3. Have you changed your word processor to insert curly quotes instead of straight quotes, and removed any instances of straight quotes?
4. Have you chosen a style of dash? Have you used it properly?
5. Are you using italics in the right places? Or too much?
6. Are your paragraph indents formatted? Have you removed all tabs?
7. Have you removed all your double spaces, and cleaned the spaces off the ends of your paragraphs?

2.3

TITLES & CHAPTER HEADINGS

These are easy to forget. Even I forget and remember at the last minute to make sure they are consistent. We are always so focussed on polishing the actual story that simple, yet very important, things like headings get overlooked.

TITLES

Your book is going to look amateurish if there is a typo in your title. Not only that, you will be extremely ashamed of yourself.

I've never had a typo in my title before, but I did have a typo in an author quote on the cover of one of my books. Within the quote, *deep* was spelled *deap*. And I didn't notice until a friend of mine emailed me. Can you imagine the hassle I went through to change one letter on the cover and re-upload it to all the retailers? What a nightmare. My lesson was learned.

Don't make the same mistake. Read your title, and cover copy carefully. Multiple times. Have friends check it for you. Sometimes you will not see things because your brain is filling in the blanks. You are so used to knowing what it's meant to be.

CHAPTER HEADINGS

Two words that I keep repeating over and over in this book are: be consistent. Can you imagine how embarrassing it would be to have chapter headings that varied in format and style like this?

Chapter 1
Chapter two
Chapter Three
chapter 4
chapter five
chapter Six
Seven
EIGHT
nine
10
Chapter Eleven
Chapter Twelve
Chapter Thirteen
<u>Chapter Fourteen</u>

Get the picture? I've never seen a book with this much inconsistency, but I have seen a book that switched between two or three of these styles. Maybe readers didn't notice, but being an editor, I did, and it really stood out. Better to be safe than ... er ... embarrassed.

So ... make sure they are all exactly the same in every single chapter. Same applies for chapters that are titled. Be sure that they are styled and formatted in exactly the same way.

The most efficient way to check this is to divide your printed manuscript at the beginning of each chapter, and lay them out on a table so they are all visible at the same time. You will be able to see immediately where the inconsistencies are. Mark the changes on the manuscript with pen and then put the changes through on the computer. If you don't mark them up, you run the risk of getting confused and changing something to the opposite of what you had intended when scrolling through your Word document. Trust me. It happens. *Raises hand.*

Note: If you know how to set up *Styles* in Word, you won't have any problems with this.

Checklist:
1. Are there any typos in your cover copy?
2. Are your chapter headings all styled the same way?

2.4

FRONT MATTER, END MATTER, ACKNOWLEDGEMENTS, BACK COVER BLURB

These too are things that many write quickly and fail to proofread properly. Gosh, even I published the all-in-one edition of the *Writing in a Nutshell* series with a typo in the blurb. How? Because I did it way too quickly and at the last minute and, even though I had two friends look at it for me, for some reason they didn't notice either. It must have been one of those things that writers autocorrect in their heads while reading and it therefore didn't stick out.

I discovered the typo when I submitted the book information and cover art to an advertising site a whole week after it was officially released. It was way past midnight when I noticed it, and I had a heart attack. It wasn't a major typo, but it was in a *writing* skills book. How embarrassing! I stayed up very late that night making sure I changed it everywhere. And that included a lot of retailers, my website, and sites like Goodreads. Don't put yourself through the torture. Don't be impatient. Let these things sit for a few days so you can look at them with fresh eyes. It will save you time—and panic!—in the long run.

FRONT MATTER

What does the front matter consist of? Well, it can vary, but I'm going to tell you based on what is typically done, and in the order it's done. This isn't set in stone, but it's what I think looks best in a paperback.

1.   Praise for *Title of Book*

I put this on the very first page of the book after the front cover. I make sure I include enough text to fill one page. This is going to differ depending on the trim size of your book, and the type and size of the font used. So if you intend to put *Praise* in the front matter, make sure you collect enough. You can always trim them down.

Example quote:

"A tightly plotted read with fascinating characters, Bitter Like Orange Peel *compels readers to unravel the layers of intertwining stories until the shocking core is revealed."* *—Talli Roland, bestselling author*

Tip: Do not assume that because these quotes were written by others that there aren't going to be any errors in them. They need to be proofread with the same level of focus as anything else in the book.

2.   About the Author

It's nice to include a short biography on the third page, leaving page two blank.

3.   Also by *Author Name*

On the verso of the biography page—page four—I list all
other books I've written under category headings, i.e. *Fiction*,
Nonfiction, *Poetry*.

4.   Title Page 1

This is like a less-detailed version of your front cover inside
the book. I usually put this on page five.

5.   Imprint Page (aka Credits)

I put this on page six. The information on this page varies
with different publishers and authors, but this is how it looks
in my latest novel:

BITTER LIKE ORANGE PEEL

Copyright © 2013 Jessica Bell
All rights reserved.
ISBN: 978-0-9875931-2-2

Published by Vine Leaves Press 2013
Melbourne, Vic, Australia

No parts of this publication may be reproduced, stored in a retrieval system,
or transmitted in any form or by any means, electronic, mechanical, photo-
copying, recording, or otherwise, without the prior written permission of the
copyright owner.

This book is sold subject to the condition that it shall not, by way of trade
or otherwise, be lent, resold, hired out, or otherwise circulated without the
publisher's prior consent in any form of binding or cover other than that in
which it is published and without a similar condition including this condition being imposed on the subsequent purchaser. Under no circumstances
may any part of this book be photocopied for resale.

This is a work of fiction. Any similarity between the characters and situations
within its pages and places or persons, living or dead, is unintentional and
co-incidental.

Cover Photography from Shutterstock.com
Cover design: Jessica Bell
Interior design: Amie McCracken

6.   Dedication

I put this on the following page—page seven—and it pretty much speaks for itself. I'm sure you've all seen these in other books you've read. It could be something as simple as *For John*, or it could be a little more detailed and include a reason why. Some people include quotes from other authors that are symbolically relevant to their story. Whatever you do choose to put here, make sure it is centered and the only thing on the page. It's special.

7.   Title Page 2

You don't have to add this. I didn't in my last book, but I wish I did. Some other books I've read have it. It serves as a reminder of what is being read before launching into the story. Make sure this second title page is on the right side of the spread, with the left side blank. It looks cleaner that way. Also, it's cleaner to start the first chapter on the next right page, leaving the verso of the second title page blank, too.

Do I have to remind you to proofread all this front matter properly? Nah …

Note: The general rule with eBooks is that, save for the title page, all of the front matter goes to the back of the book so that downloadable samples are of the actual story. EBooks can include clickable links to pages where book reviews can be added, a sign-up page to your newsletter, and links to purchase your backlist, too.

END MATTER

There are a lot of things you can include in the back of your book.

Here are some common things:
- Acknowledgements
- A suggestion to sign up to your author newsletter
- A call to connect with you on your website or other social media platforms
- A call to post a review
- Adverts for your backlist or upcoming titles
- Sample excerpts from your forthcoming titles
- An author interview
- Book club discussion questions

There is no standard way to set any of these things out. Just be creative. And proofread them!

ACKNOWLEDGEMENTS

I always forget about this until the last minute, and then struggle to recall who had helped me with the production of my book. It's a good idea to keep a list of people who helped you along the way from the get-go, so when you do reach this point, you are not frazzled.

The people I have forgotten have all been lovely about it, but I'm pretty sure I've hurt some feelings. I forgot to acknowledge my parents in my first ever published book, *Twisted Velvet Chains*. It was months before I was able to live it down.

Even friends of my parents were asking me why I didn't acknowledge them. It was quite a topic of conversation on the little island where my parents live. I have never forgotten to mention them since.\

Who should you include? Here are a few ideas: beta readers, proofreaders, editors, people who have reviewed a preview copy, cover designer, partners, any permissions given to use quotes (poetry, song lyrics, etc.), reference books, biographies, websites you have used for research, etc, people who have shared their life stories and allowed you to use their anecdotes.

Note: This is also a great sales tool as those acknowledged have immediate buy in and will be the most lively promoters of your book.

BACK COVER BLURB

Okay, I know that this isn't going to go *in* your manuscript, but as I pointed out in "Titles & Chapter Headings," you do not want to make mistakes with this.

Write it early. Let it sit. Rewrite it. Let it sit. Have friends read it. Let it sit. Give it time to mature. Proofread it. Proofread it again. Then it will be perfect by the time you are ready to put it on your cover and websites. Wait! Proofread it a couple more times once it's on the cover too. Things can happen during the transfer from manuscript to design program.

Checklist:
1. Have you organized your front and end matter?
2. Have you included everyone in your acknowledgements?
3. Is your back cover blurb in tiptop shape?

PART THREE

WE ALL MAKE MISTAKES.
THE KEY IS TO
learn FROM THEM.

Now that I've helped you polish your novel, and you probably feel like absolutely everything is in order, and there isn't even one error left to taint your manuscript, I've got two more words for you:

Think again.

This chapter is all about making you feel good, while simultaneously making you feel helpless. Sorry about that. But I do want you to see that you are not alone in this.

As you know, I've experienced quite a few of my own editorial blunders. In fact, there have been a lot more than the instances I've mentioned in this book. Because you know what? There is always something. There is always going to be something that slips through. And that is a fact with traditionally published books, too.

I found one in a novel I recently read (I won't name it!), that said something like "I calling her." And this was a *reprint* of a book that was originally published ten years ago. Imagine how many extra edits this book went through, and the error still slipped in.

I repeat: There will always be something. The only thing you can do is minimize the errors as best you can.

I thought you might appreciate some concrete proof of this, so asked a few authors I know to answer the following question:

What is the biggest mistake you noticed in a book you previously published, that you will never forget, and now have a keen eye for?

So, that's it from me. I hope you enjoyed this book. If enjoying a book about editing is at all possible!

Over to you, folks:

Samantha Warren, from *samantha-warren.com*

"In my paranormal romance (which went through a content editor, seven beta readers, and a proofreader), I kept using the word *ephemeral* when I wanted to say *ethereal*. No one noticed until I published it. The very first reviewer sent me an email and pointed it out. So much egg on my face. I'd also like to share what eventually got me into writing in the first place. I was reading through the Dark Elf trilogy, a traditionally published, well-loved series, and found twelve mistakes in ten pages. It made me crazy. I decided I wanted to be an editor and promptly switched my major from Computer Science to English. I'm not an editor, but that definitely was the starting point on my way to being a writer."

Derek Murphy, from *creativindie.com*

"In my first book, I used *thrown* instead of *throne* twice. It earned me a lot of criticism."

Sandra Schwab, from *sandraschwab.com*

"In my second novel, *Castle of the Wolf*, I used the name *Ferdinand* for my hero's father and one of the servants. In the very same novel a horse disappears: my heroine is driven in a small carriage from an inn to the castle she has inherited. At the inn, the carriage is drawn by two horses. By the time they reach the castle, there is only one horse left. (But hey, that story is set in the Black Forest—*any*thing can happen in these dark, dark woods!)"

Joe Cawley, from *joecawley.co.uk*

"In my first memoir, *More Ketchup than Salsa*, one chapter featured a local gangster—name changed obviously. Two months after it hit the bookshelves, a reader pointed out that I'd used his real name in one instance. This was despite the book being run through the edit/proofing grinder of a publishing company. Needless to say I got it changed PDQ. I also kept a low profile for a while."

Jan Ruth, from *janruth.com*

"I couldn't believe how many brains were confused by Brian, and how much sand my characters ate for dessert in *Silver Rain*."

Emily White, from *emilytwhite.blogspot.com*

"In my debut novel, *Elemental*, I put too much of myself into the cover instead of what it should have reflected: my book and the audience I wanted to target. Instead of coming off as a dark, slightly campy space opera, I'd attracted lovers of paranormal romance. I'm still trying to work my way out of that mess, but after a lot of patience, a lot of work, and a new cover, I'm finally inching my way into that niche market I should have worked towards in the beginning. The good news is I taught myself that, yes, I absolutely needed a target audience, and that, yes, things have been done for years because they work."

Kathryn Magendie, from *kathrynmagendie.com*

"I know that no matter how much of an editing process my work goes through, it's extremely difficult to get by without any error at all, even if it's only one that the author herself notices. I'm a perfectionist, so an 'error' no one may notice but me, will still make me think, 'Dang it!' Worse, any blatant error—like in my first published novel, *Tender Graces,* where there was a missing period, but up farther on the page there were two periods, as if one period ran up to be with the other one! Or in the second book, *Secret Graces*, when Virginia Kate wanted strawberry jam, but on the next page she ate blueberry (okay, maybe she changed her mind!)—is like a knife in the gut to me, so I do everything in my power to make sure those kinds of things do not happen. Yet, what I learned after my first novel, that perhaps isn't a 'mistake' in the terms of typos or over-looked wrangly things, is that I don't need so many words; I don't need to keep every sentence or paragraph that I think just has to be in there—they don't. With each novel following *Tender Graces*, my books become less wordy. With a keen eye and experience, I am learning the art of the delete key."

Walt Morton, from *waltmorton.com*

"I don't have a specific mistake, but early on my process was muddled. Do not confuse the editing of a novel with the proofing. Editing you may still be changing a lot of things. Proofing the story is 'locked' and you are just cleaning up presentation. If you are not clear about that—you will end up having to re-start proofing efforts. Do not think that spell-checking programs, other proofing efforts or even three professional proofreaders will catch every error. One of the most insidious errors is a repeated word that may develop in typing/editing in a sentence like: 'He sat on on the bed.' Everybody can miss a thing like that especially if it's on a line break. Read your finished document on at least three other devices other than what you wrote it on (paper, Kindle, iPhone, etc). And when you are really done make a 'final master' file that reflects exactly the edition currently for sale on Amazon. That way, if six months out, a reader points out a typo on page 423 it is not all that hard to update the fix."

Joe Cottonwood, from *joecottonwood.com*

"On page one of my novel, published by a prestigious NY publisher in 1981: *My own first car was a '54 Chevy Bel Air. She was a stick V-8.* Chevy did not produce a V-8 until 1955. Minor matter? No-o-o-o. People howled."

Liz Kales, from *about.me/lizkalesauthor*

"My main character's name is *Marc* (he's French). About half way through the book, there is one chapter where I call him *Mark* two or three times. I never noticed it, but some of the readers sure did."

Rebecca Lang, from *twitter.com/Rebecca_Lang*

"I once edited a friend's story in which the magic object changed twice—from a book to a chalice. When I pointed this out she said 'but it's supposed to be a wand!'"

Jeannie van Rompaey, from *jeannievanrompaey.com*

"A case of show and tell. I showed a character red in the face, tearing up a note and then said she was angry. Urgh! We have to learn to trust our readers."

Helen Hollick, from *www.helenhollick.net*

"How about this as a sharp learning-curve lesson? Having been mainstream published for many years it didn't occur to me that an Assisted Indie Company would not typeset my first indie-produced novel correctly. I submitted the text in Comic Sans—and they printed it that way. Unfortunately these were not proof copies: the first time I saw them was on launch day at my local bookshop. I was horrified. I managed to get a reprint done, and the lesson is—always check a final version in hard copy book-format if possible, (PDF if not) before officially publishing. The quality of the production of your novel reflects the quality of your writing."

Althea Hayton

"I made up a biography of an eighty-six-year-old, using his words and over one hundred photos (just as a favour). Edited it with enormous care, but in the end felt too poorly and exhausted to do any more. Got it done by Lightning Source and he made the first order with immense excitement, until he gave me a copy, and there on the spine I had spelt his name wrong! *blush* He was very kind about it. If he ever wants any more I'll pay for a second proof to be made—but, oh dear!"

Alex J. Cavanaugh, from *alexjcavanaugh.com*

"My first book, *CassaStar*, passed through my test readers and publisher's editors without any of us noticing that I had spelled *hangar* wrong. It was spelled *hanger* (for clothes) instead of *hangar* (for aircraft). We caught it by the second book, *CassaFire*, but thousands had already seen the mistake in the first one before it was corrected. Hey, all I can do is laugh about it now. And never spell the word wrong again!"

Magdalena Ball, from *magdalenaball.com*

"The publisher for three of my books went bust, and handed back all my 'ready to publish' files to me. They'd all been professionally proofread and edited, and I just wanted to get them back on Amazon for sale as quickly as possible as they were still selling (the last book had only been released a few months earlier).

"So I converted them to print through CreateSpace and Kindle, and carefully proofread a printed galley I had sent to myself. It all looked fine, so I put them on sale and went about my business. Until I started getting reviews on Amazon referencing the number of errors.

"I quickly looked through my printed version and couldn't find those errors. Then I checked the Kindle version, only to realize that, in the conversion, the manuscript had lost a number of words that were almost impossible to find without doing a very thorough read-through. Words like *it*, *and*, and *if* were missing—just left out of the Kindle version. I had to take the Kindle version down, re-do the whole thing, which took me many hours, and re-set it up with a clean copy.

"The version there now is a good one, with the errors fixed up, but the negative reviews remain there indefinitely, as a reminder to me to never assume what looks okay in one format, will work in another, and to always check and recheck before pressing that publish button."

Clarissa Draper

"I try to be as accurate as possible when it comes to describing murder scenes and forensic concepts in my mystery novels. However, after the first novel in my mystery series was published, a reviewer pointed out a mistake I had made with regards to crime scene and timeline management. How embarrassing! Now I read all the investigative manuals I can to make sure the terms, concepts, and techniques described in my novels are explained accurately."

PK Hrezo, from *twitter.com/pkhrezo*

"I thought getting a proofreader for my debut novel, *Butterman (Time) Travel, Inc.*, was the final tweak. What I wish I had done, is re-read the entire story AFTER correcting errors from the proofreader. You'd never believe how many she missed! Just goes to show that we ALL make mistakes and miss them too! It was after I already had my book launch that I found more typos and errors. Even after multiple critiques, beta reads, editing, AND a proofreader, these were missed. Next time I'll take the time to go through the book one more time before launch."

Cherie Reich, from *cheriereich.webs.com*

"Although contracted by two publishers, but only published with one of them, my horror novelette had a mistake that two editors, two proofreaders, two critique partners, myself, and multiple readers missed every single time. I had written *peaked* when it should've been *piqued*. I don't think I even knew there was a difference until I came across the words on a blog talking about common errors, and I still didn't realize I'd made the mistake in my own book until I'd gotten my rights back and decided to edit it one more time before self-publishing it. As soon as I saw the word, heat flooded my face. Oh my goodness, a thousand plus people had purchased and possibly read the novelette and yet no one ever mentioned, or possibly noticed, the wrong word. Whether I'm editing my own work or someone else's, I have certain words and phrases I note down to make certain they're correct. Although I take comfort that maybe no one noticed, it just goes to show we sometimes read what we think things should be."

Debbie Young, from *authordebbieyoung.com*

"My biggest disaster (the one that I've spotted, anyway) was when producing a prospectus for a PR client, which had taken months to prepare and fine-tune. Then when the final, final, final proofread was done and I was sick of the sight of it and word-blind to any further changes, I realized we hadn't added the credit for the photographer, whose stunning photos made it so beautiful. I asked the graphic designer, who had introduced me to the photographer in the first place, and who lived next door to him, to add the credit line, but said no need to run that past me. I hadn't realized that the designer, though brilliant with design, was not so great with words. He spelt the photographer's name wrong—very wrong. Cue sleepless nights of remorse for something that really should not have happened. Not exactly a self-publishing story, as it was a commercial print job, but I feel better for sharing it, nearly twenty years after the event!"

Jim Murdoch, from *jimmurdoch.co.uk*

"Editing can't be rushed. You need distance to be able to do that. The Israeli novelist Aharon Appelfeld hides each finished manuscript in a drawer for two or three years before returning to prune it further. That may seem like an eternity, but I think it's essential. You cannot put on your editor's hat while still wearing your writer's hat. You need to divorce yourself from the material, and the best way to accomplish that is to move on to your next project.

"I had my first novel professionally edited by a reputable firm. It wasn't cheap. They say you get what you pay for but that's not necessarily the case. I made a half-hearted effort to find a traditional publisher but then life got in the way and I wound up working on other stuff. Years later, having decided to publish independently, I sent copies to three friends—all writers—for their input. All three found things the professional should've caught. My wife, who edited her own literary journals for some twenty years, also gave the book a final once-over and made fixes. So you can imagine my mortification when I posted out finished copies and reviewers still found some half-dozen typos.

"There's a precept I live by now: My name on the cover, my

responsibility. I still involve others in the process—never hurts to get a second, third, or even a fourth set of eyes to look at your work—but I'm always the last person to proofread my books before they go off to the printer. I devoted months to editing my last book. I went through it with a fine tooth comb seventeen times before handing it over to my wife and then read it twice more afterwards before deciding we were good to go."

Rachel Morgan, from *rachel-morgan.com*

"In my third *Creepy Hollow* book, *The Faerie War*, there is quite a prominent secondary character named Jamon. Several months after publication, one of my friends read this book, and when she was done she sent me an email. 'Who's Jalen?' she asked, referencing a particular page. I thought, 'Seriously? This character is mentioned all over the place. It isn't possible for her not to know who he is.' Then the overly harsh light bulb turned on, and I remembered that the character in question was named *Jamon*, not *Jalen*. Jalen was a character from a completely different book (an unpublished one), and he had no business being anywhere near *Creepy Hollow*! How embarrassing! Neither my beta readers, my editor, my proofreader nor any of the HUNDREDS of readers who read *The Faerie War* before this particular friend did, noticed and/or mentioned this mistake! The lesson? Don't let your eyes skim over ANYTHING when checking your work: even the characters' names!"

L. Diane Wolfe, from *spunkonastick.net*

"In the beginning, I relied too much on the passive word 'was' and I head-hopped. A lot! My publisher's editor tamed some of that mess, but it still showed in the beginning of my *The Circle of Friends* series. Fortunately, the more we write, the more experience we gain. I know to watch for those issues, and better yet, I know how to fix them. (And a sign by my computer that says 'Stop the WASes!' helps, too.)"

India Drummond, from *indiadrummond.com*

"Fortunately, I've always hired a freelance editor and she's kept me from publishing some of my most embarrassing mistakes, such as not knowing the difference between *discrete* and *discreet*. I did have a reviewer on one of my early books write and tell me that she loved my book, but she got so annoyed by my constant use of the phrase 'he couldn't help but…' As soon as she said it, I realized how right she was! I use *autocrit.com* to check for repeated phrases in close proximity, but because I do it chapter by chapter, I never thought to check for how often a particular phrase was used over an entire book. I went through and edited that one and I try to be more careful about crutch expressions like that now!"

Did you find any errors in this book? If you did, stop laughing and let me know what they are by email. Because you've won yourself a free book!

You can find my contact details on my website: *jessicabellauthor.com*

RECOMMENDED READING

WRITING CRAFT

Writing in a Nutshell books, by ME!
Nail Your Novel books, by Roz Morris
Go Creative! books, by Orna Ross
The Emotion Thesaurus, The Positive Trait Thesaurus, & *The Negative Trait Thesaurus,* by Angela Ackermann and Becca Puglisi
Structuring Your Novel, by K.M. Weiland

EDITING

Say What? The Fiction Writer's Handy Guide to Grammar, Punctuation, and Word Usage, by C.S. Lakin

PUBLISHING

The Triskele Trail: A Pathway to Independent Publishing, by the authors at Triskele Books
Choosing a Self-Publishing Service, by Alliance of Independent Authors
The Successful Author Mindset, by Joanna Penn

If you found this book helpful, it would be extremely appreciated if you could post a review at the retailer you purchased it from.

Interested in my upcoming titles?
You can sign up for my newsletter at
jessicabellauthor.com *to stay up-to-date.*

Independent Publishing Assistance

All your book production needs at your fingertips.

www.indiepublishingassist.com

www.ingramcontent.com/pod-product-compliance
Lightning Source LLC
Chambersburg PA
CBHW030025290326
41934CB00005B/496